JUL 0 7 2004

WORLD WATCH

UNITED NATIONS

Stewart Ross

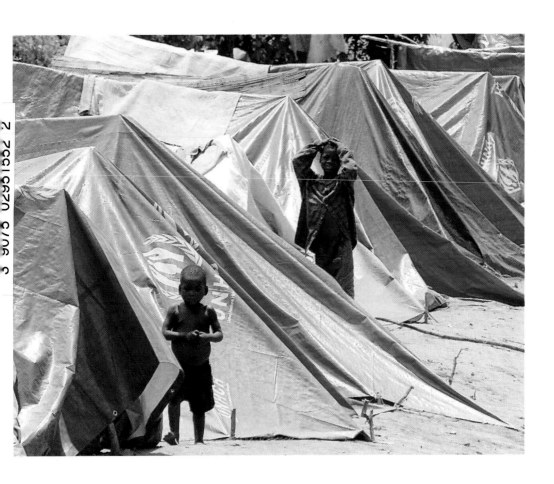

Raintree

Chicago, Illinois

WORLDWATCH SERIES

Greenpeace • The Red Cross Movement • UNICEF
• United Nations • World Health Organization • WWF

© 2004 Raintree
Published by Raintree, a division of Reed Elsevier, Inc., Chicago, Illinois
Customer Service 888-363-4266
Visit our website at www.raintreelibrary.com

Copyright Permissions
Raintree
100 N. LaSalle, Suite 1200
Chicago, IL 60602

Library of Congress Cataloging-in-Publication Data:
Ross, Stewart.
  United Nations / Stewart Ross.
    v. cm. -- (World watch)
Includes bibliographical references and index.
Contents: Blue helmets -- World government? -- A troubled history --
Striving for peace -- Rights and wrongs -- Working together -- The
shared environment -- Future uncertain.
  ISBN 0-7398-6616-8 (Library Binding-hardcover)
  1. United Nations--Juvenile literature. [1. United Nations.] I.
Title. II. Series: World watch (Chicago, Ill.)
  JZ4984.6.R67 2004
  341.23'09--dc21   2003006092

Printed in Hong Kong by Wing King Tong.
1 2 3 4 5 6 7 8 9 0 09 08 07 06 05 04

Picture acknowledgments: Cover Topham; title page Popperfoto; p. 4 Topham Picturepoint; p. 5 H. Davies/Exile Images; p. 6 Topham Picturepoint; p. 7 Topham Picturepoint; p. 8 Novosti/Topham; p. 11 Popperfoto/Reuters; p .12 Mark Ludak/Topham/Image Works; p. 13 Teit Hornbak/Still Pictures; p. 13 Figures in table: www.globalpolicy.org; p. 14 Popperfoto; p. 15 Popperfoto; p. 16 Popperfoto; p. 17 J. Holmes/Exile Images; p. 18 Pascal Guyot/Poppperfoto; p. 20 Popperfoto; p. 21 Topham Picturepoint; p. 22 Topham/AP; p. 23 Popperfoto; p 24 Eric Feferberg/Popperfoto; p, 26 (top) Topham/AP; p, 26 (bottom) Universal Pictorial Press/Topham; p, 28 Mark Edwards/Still Pictures; p 29 Topham Picturepoint; p. 30 Popperfoto; p. 31 Jerry Lampen/ Popperfoto/Reuters; p. 32 Popperfoto; p. 33 H. Davies/Exile Images; p. 35 Popperfoto; p. 36 Popperfoto; p. 37 H. Davies/Exile Images; p. 39 John Isaac/Still Pictures; p. 40 Oliver Langrand/Still Pictures; p. 41 Mike Hutchings/Popperfoto/Reuters; p. 42 Mike Segar/Popperfoto/Reuters; p. 43 Popperfoto; p. 44 Topham/UN; p. 45 Peter Morgan/Popperfoto/Reuters.

Cover: A United Nations Spanish armored personnel carrier on patrol in Mostar, Bosnia, in 2000.

CONTENTS

Chapter One:
Blue Helmets

• •

The 11-year-old boy cautiously lifted his head above the window sill and stared out into the village street. A tank! Mohammed had never seen one before. He gazed in wonder as the machine clanked slowly past.

"What is it, Mohammed?" called his mother. "What's that noise?"

"It's a tank, Mama," the boy replied. "Enormous. With men in blue helmets on top."

"Blue helmets? Are you sure?"

"Yes, Mama. Who are they?"

"Blue helmets means the United Nations, Mohammed. Soldiers sent to protect us. To keep the peace."

The boy turned back into the room. "What peace, Mama?" he frowned.

"How can they keep the peace when there isn't any?"

"I don't know," replied his mother softly. "And I'm not sure they do, either."

UNPROFOR

This scene, and many like it, took place in Bosnia. Until the 1990s, Bosnia had been part of Yugoslavia, a large country in southeastern Europe. During a long civil war, Yugoslavia broke up into several separate states. Bosnia was one of them.

• •

Soldiers of the UN Protection Force are welcomed by Bosnians as they arrive in Pale, near the Bosnian capital Sarajevo, in 1992. ▼

The United Nations (UN) is an association of 191 countries that have joined together for their mutual benefit, especially to promote peace. In 1992 it sent a protection force—named UNPROFOR—to try to create a no-fighting zone between the warring forces in Bosnia. It was never quite clear how UNPROFOR could do this. It was not equipped to fight and, as Mohammed realized, it could not keep a peace that did not exist.

The blue helmets

The UN does not have armed forces of its own. Whenever troops are needed, the UN calls on its member states to provide them and pays for their use. The forces keep their own commanders, although supreme

▲ Bosnians begin to repair the damage to the city of Sarajevo soon after the Bosnian war.

command rests (in theory) with the head of the UN, the secretary-general. UN forces are on loan. Their first loyalty is to their own country, and they can be withdrawn at any time. As a result, UN forces do not normally do more than observe and help civilians caught up in the fighting. UNPROFOR, for instance, did not stop the slaughter in Bosnia. Many other branches of the UN share UNPROFOR's problems. Their aims are excellent, but carrying them out is often extremely difficult.

"A 1994 report by the UN identified no fewer than 187 suspected mass-grave sites in former Yugoslavia, most of them in Bosnia. Thirteen supposedly had '500 bodies or more,' and some as many as 5,000. The report came out a year before the fall of Srebrenica ... following which up to 8,000 Muslim men, women, and children vanished."

A quote from *Time* magazine (January 29, 1996) illustrating how ineffective UNPROFOR forces were

Chapter Two:
World Government?

During World War I (1914–1918), about 13 million people were killed in combat, and many times this number were injured. The fighting devastated vast areas of Europe, caused numerous civilian deaths, smashed empires, and brought down governments.

Before the war ended, U.S. President Woodrow Wilson came up with a plan to prevent such horror from ever happening again. His idea was to form a League of Nations—a sort of club to which all states could belong. Its rules would make sure that disputes were settled peacefully, bringing in a new era of harmony between the nations of the world.

A failed attempt

In practice, the League of Nations was a failure. Several powerful states, including Russia and President Wilson's own United States, refused to join. Member countries found that the league had no way of making uncooperative governments obey its rules. In 1923 Italy's fascist dictator Mussolini defied the league's wishes, and Japan did the same in 1931. By 1933, when Hitler took Nazi Germany out of the league, the organization was just about finished.

◀ In this cartoon the League of Nations (the rabbit), with no access to armed forces, is seen as powerless to stop fights between nations (the snake).

British Prime Minister Winston Churchill (left, foreground) and U.S. President Franklin D. Roosevelt (right) meet on the warship USS *Augusta* to discuss the Atlantic Charter. ▶

The Atlantic Charter

The conflicts that began World War II started in Europe in 1939. Losses and destruction threatened to be even greater than in World War I, and leaders wondered what had gone wrong with the League of Nations. They planned a new, more powerful organization.

In 1941, before the United States was at war, President F. D. Roosevelt and British Prime Minister Winston Churchill drew up a document known as the Atlantic Charter. The charter called for a new organization to replace the League of Nations. It was the beginning of the United Nations.

The road to San Francisco

In 1942, 26 countries accepted the Atlantic Charter and signed a Declaration of the United Nations. The discussions, led by the United States, the Soviet Union (USSR), and Britain, continued until April 25, 1945, when 50 nations met for a conference in San Francisco, California.

After two months of talks, the conference accepted a charter, a document that set out the principles and structure of the United Nations Organization (UNO). All the countries at the conference signed the charter, and four months later the UN came into being.

❝We the people of the United Nations, determined to save succeeding generations from the scourge of war ... and to reaffirm faith in fundamental human rights ... in the equal rights of men and women and of nations large and small, and ... to unite our strength to maintain peace and security, and ... to employ international machinery for the promotion of the economic and social advancement of all peoples, have ... agreed to the present Charter of the United Nations.❞

The opening words of the UN charter

The General Assembly

The central body of the United Nations is a kind of world parliament known as the General Assembly. It debates many issues, from pollution to terrorism, but has no direct power to get things done. It can only recommend action to other bodies like the Security Council (see pages 9–11). In 1967, for instance, the assembly passed a resolution demanding that Israel withdraw from captured Arab territories, but Israel has not yet done so.

Membership

All UN member states have a seat in the General Assembly. UN membership has almost quadrupled since 1945, for two reasons. First, some countries, such as the Soviet Union, have divided up to create more countries. Second, the ending of European empires after World War II led to the formation of many new nations. In 1960, for instance, the newly independent African countries Benin, Cameroon, Chad, Congo, Gabon, Madagascar, Mali, and Nigeria all joined the UN.

▲ A meeting of the UN General Assembly in 1969. At this meeting the UN accepted a resolution to eliminate all forms of racial discrimination.

The General Assembly decides to admit new members after the Security Council has recommended them. The assembly has the power to suspend or expel a member, although this has never happened. Disputes over whether countries should be allowed to join are quite common. Arab nations, for example, want Palestine to join, but other countries do not see Palestine as a country and so, do not want it to join.

The assembly in action

The General Assembly meets every year, from September to December, in New York. The assembly may meet at other times to discuss a crisis, as it did in 2001 when Israel sent troops into Palestinian towns in response to Palestinian bombings within Israel.

Each nation has one vote. This gives a tiny Pacific island state like Tuvalu (population 10,000) the same voting power as China (population 1.26 billion). This is why the assembly has no executive (action-taking) power. If it did, a majority of small states would be able to force their will on big countries with much larger populations. Also, groups of states would be able to join together against ones they disliked.

The votes of two-thirds of member states are needed to pass resolutions (decisions) on important matters like peace and UN spending. There are six official UN languages: Arabic, Chinese, English, French, Russian, and Spanish. All speeches are translated while they are given. The assembly has seven main committees that carry out much of its work.

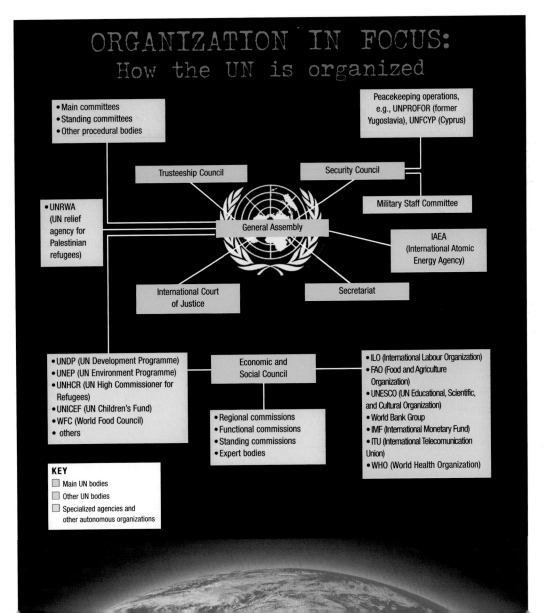

ORGANIZATION IN FOCUS:
How the UN is organized

- Main committees
- Standing committees
- Other procedural bodies

Peacekeeping operations, e.g., UNPROFOR (former Yugoslavia), UNFCYP (Cyprus)

Trusteeship Council

Security Council

Military Staff Committee

- UNRWA (UN relief agency for Palestinian refugees)

General Assembly

IAEA (International Atomic Energy Agency)

International Court of Justice

Secretariat

- UNDP (UN Development Programme)
- UNEP (UN Environment Programme)
- UNHCR (UN High Commissioner for Refugees)
- UNICEF (UN Children's Fund)
- WFC (World Food Council)
- others

Economic and Social Council

- ILO (International Labour Organization)
- FAO (Food and Agriculture Organization)
- UNESCO (UN Educational, Scientific, and Cultural Organization)
- World Bank Group
- IMF (International Monetary Fund)
- ITU (International Telecommunication Union)
- WHO (World Health Organization)

- Regional commissions
- Functional commissions
- Standing commissions
- Expert bodies

KEY
- Main UN bodies
- Other UN bodies
- Specialized agencies and other autonomous organizations

The Security Council

The Security Council is the branch of the UN responsible for international peace and security. The victorious nations from World War II—the United States, Britain, France, the USSR (now Russia), and China—suggested creating the Security Council and made themselves its permanent members.

As well as these five permanent members, the council had six rotating additional members, who were elected by the General Assembly every two years. The number of additional members rose to ten in 1963. In 2003 the additional members were Angola, Bulgaria, Cameroon, Chile, Germany, Guinea, Mexico, Pakistan, Spain, and Syria.

The presidency of the Security Council changes each month. The council usually meets at UN headquarters in New York, but occasionally it meets elsewhere. In February 1972, for example, it met in Addis Ababa, Ethiopia, to discuss the subject of apartheid in South Africa (see page 29).

The council at work

Security Council meetings are normally more exciting than those of the General Assembly. It is smaller—just fifteen delegates (representatives) around a horseshoe-shaped table—and it is always in session. Member nations must have a delegate based in the UN building ready to go to a Security Council meeting at any time of the day or night.

Unlike the General Assembly, the Security Council has real power to do things. It recommends new UN member states, puts forward new secretaries-general, and tells members to take action against those who break UN rules. It is the only UN body that can demand military action (see pages 14 and 18). All UN members must carry out Security Council decisions. There is a safeguard, however. All permanent members of the Council have a veto, which means that they can block a decision, even if everyone else is in favor (see page 14). Some observers believe the United States's economic power allows it to unfairly dominate the Security Council.

Anti-terrorism committee

A dramatic example of the power of the United States followed the terrorist attacks of September 11, 2001. The New York attacks also had a special effect on the UN because they took place not far from UN headquarters.

On September 28 the Security Council complied with U.S. wishes and passed a resolution that condemned terrorism (as defined by the United States) and all means of supporting it. It also set up a special committee of the council to see that member states reported within 90 days that they had obeyed this resolution.

The face of modern terrorism. On September 11, 2001, two airplanes were hijacked and crashed into the twin towers of the World Trade Center in New York. ▼

Running the UN

The UN secretary-general is responsible for the day-to-day running of the UN. It is a near-impossible job. Secretaries-general have to be administrators, diplomats, and spokespeople for everyone in the world, especially those people whose voices are not normally heard. To help, the post of deputy secretary-general was created in 1998. Louise Fréchette (Canada) was the first deputy secretary-general.

Secretaries-general come from countries not linked to the great powers. They have been from Norway (Trygve Lie, appointed 1946), Sweden (Dag Hammarskjöld, 1953), Burma (U Thant, 1961), Austria (Kurt Waldheim, 1972), Peru (Pérez de Cuéllar, 1982), Egypt (Boutros Boutros-Ghali, 1992) and Nigeria (Kofi Annan, 1997). All were recommended to the Security Council by their native countries. They serve a maximum of two four-year terms.

The UN career of Boutros Boutros-Ghali, an ex-deputy prime minister of Egypt and a well-known scholar, shows the difficulties a secretary-general can face. He tried to keep the UN independent after the Cold War (see pages 18–19). In particular, he was worried about the growing influence of the United States over the UN. He resisted U.S. calls for cuts in UN spending, and in 1996 the U.S. stopped him from being re-elected. His successor, Kofi Annan, immediately began the proposed cost- cutting measures.

The Secretariat

The secretary-general heads the Secretariat, a permanent staff of 8,900 civil servants from about 160 countries. They work in New York, Addis Ababa, Bangkok, Beirut, Geneva, Nairobi, Santiago, and Vienna. Other workers are hired for special tasks, such as delivering aid.

The range of UN workers is enormous. It includes secretaries and translators, truck drivers delivering food along dusty tracks, and top-level scientists. Add to these the thousands working for other members of the UN family—such as UNICEF (the UN Children's Fund), the World Bank, and WHO (the World Health Organization)—and it becomes clear just how massive the UN is.

◀ UN Secretary-General Kofi Annan addresses the UN General Assembly in 2000.

Obviously, the UN needs money—lots of it. The 2002–2003 budget was $2.3 billion. On top of this came peacekeeping costs. In 1995 these reached a record $3 billion. A committee of contributions decides what percentage of the budget each member state should pay. This ranges from 0.01 percent for Chad to 22 percent for the United States.

UN workers in the field. In 1997 refugees fled to Thailand to avoid fighting in Cambodia. In 1999 the UNHCR provided workers and transportation to help the refugees get home. ▼

FACTFILE: Some major contributors to the UN budget, 2002

State	USA	Japan	Germany	UK	Brazil	Russia
% of UN budget	22.0	19.63	9.83	5.57	2.23	1.2
Owing from 2001	165	0	0	0	21	0
Required in 2002	283	218	109	62	23	13
Paid by end 2002	255	218	109	62	0	13
Still owing Jan 2003	193	0	0	0	44	0

(Figures are U.S.$ million)

Chapter Three:
A Troubled History

The UN, born out of war, was designed to prevent further conflict. However, even while it was being set up, there were signs of trouble ahead.

The veto

The founding members of the UN decided that the Security Council (see page 10) would be its most powerful organization. There were fears, however, that it might become too powerful. The Soviet Union (USSR) in particular, was worried that the United States might get the council to pass resolutions that would damage Soviet interests.

To stop this from happening, it was agreed that resolutions would be valid only if agreed to by every permanent council member. This gave the United States, the USSR, Britain, France, and China the power to overturn any Security Council resolution. This veto power has been very important.

Cold War

The veto was first used by the Soviet Union in February 1946. It was the beginning of 50 years of tension and misunderstanding between the United States and the USSR, a period known as the Cold War. The communist world, led by the Soviet Union and China (the East) was in opposition to the democratic-capitalist world led by the United States (the West). Each side used the veto to block the other's policy suggestions. By 1953, the Soviet Union had used the veto more than 50 times.

Before 1990, the Security Council only once agreed to take military action. It happened in 1950, when communist North Korea invaded South Korea. The Soviets did not use their veto because at the time they were refusing to attend the Security Council (see panel). In the Korean War that followed (1950–1953), the United States and its allies (fighting with UN approval) fought North Korea and, later, China. Neither side made significant long-term gains.

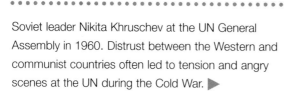

Soviet leader Nikita Khruschev at the UN General Assembly in 1960. Distrust between the Western and communist countries often led to tension and angry scenes at the UN during the Cold War. ▶

Peacekeeping

During the Cold War, the UN was not able to prevent wars. There were dozens of conflicts, large and small. What the UN did do was arrange cease-fires, keep watch in places of tension (observer missions), and place neutral troops between two hostile sides in an attempt to keep them apart (peacekeeping, see pages 22–23).

Between 1948 and 1988 the UN sent out twelve observer, or peacekeeping, forces, half of them

▲ A UNFIL soldier gives supplies to a Lebanese woman. UNFIL is a UN peacekeeping force created in 1978 to prevent conflict in Lebanon.

to the Middle East. Peacekeeping began with the UN Emergency Force in the Suez Canal region (1956). The Security Council never tried to use force to make warring parties make peace.

FACTFILE: The China Seat

In 1945 President Chiang Kai-shek's KMT party governed China. A communist revolution overthrew Chiang in 1949. He fled to Formosa (now Taiwan), insisting he was still president of China. Backed by the United States, he kept China's seat on the Security Council. The Soviets objected and temporarily boycotted (walked out of) the council. In 1971 the United States finally agreed that the China seat should go to the communist People's Republic of China.

Saving the reputation, 1945–1990

As soon as World War II broke out, politicians and scholars started asking why. The war had not been caused only by evil people; such people come to power only when conditions favor them.

These conditions were understood to be poverty, ignorance, and injustice. Therefore, the founders of the UN realized that it was not enough just to keep peace with troops and armed observers. At the same time, they had to tackle the roots of conflict.

A growing family

The UN took two steps to tackle the problems of poverty, ignorance, and injustice. First, it set up a number of funds and programs directly under the General Assembly (see organization chart, page 9). These included the Office of the UN High Commissioner for Refugees (UNHCR), established in 1950. In 1954 and 1981, UNHCR won the Nobel Peace Prize for its work with the world's homeless and stateless.

Second, to carry out its economic and social work, the UN set up the Economic and Social Council (ECOSOC, see organization chart, page 9). Originally ECOSOC had eighteen members. It kept an eye on the growing family of organizations working for a fairer and more prosperous world.

Some organizations, such as the UN Educational, Scientific, and Cultural Organization (UNESCO, see page 42), grew directly out of the UN. Others, such as the International Monetary Fund (IMF, see page 34), were only loosely part of the UN family.

A refugee camp was set up by the UNHCR in Mozambique in 2000 after floods devastated the country. ▼

Saved by UNICEF

At times during the Cold War the reputation of the UN sank very low. It failed to prevent wars and rarely did much to make peace. What was its purpose, people asked, when it seemed to be merely an expensive forum for East-West arguments?

The UN's reputation was saved by its economic and social programs. In the West its best-known symbol was the enormously popular Christmas cards produced by UNICEF (UN Children's Fund, set up in 1946 to make the world a better place for children). Worldwide sales of these cards raised millions of dollars for UNICEF's work. They also reminded people that there was more to the UN than hard-faced men in suits sitting around conference tables.

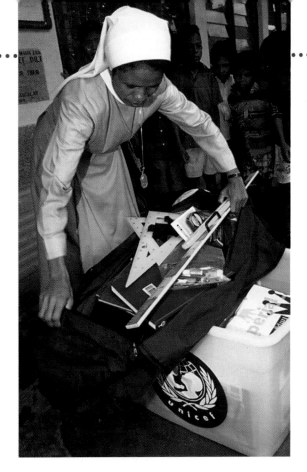

▲ East Timor became independent from Indonesia in 1999, but the struggle left the country devastated. UNICEF provided the country with more than 600 "school-in-a-box" kits, each with everything needed for a class of 80 children.

FACTFILE: UN membership

UN membership rose from 51 in 1945 to 189 in 2000. All "peace-loving" states accepting the charter are welcome, although the Security Council can veto (block) a country's application to join. For the first 15 years, the UN grew only slowly, because the United States and the USSR each rejected the inclusion of states that might side with their rivals. When the USSR and Yugoslavia broke up into their separate countries between 1990 and 1993, there was a burst of membership.

The end of the Cold War

In 1989 one of the most remarkable events of modern times began, the collapse of the communist Soviet Union. The Cold War ended at once, and Russia became a democratic, capitalist country. The states it had governed directly (for example, Ukraine) or controlled (for example, Bulgaria) became fully independent.

Meanwhile, communist China was accepting capitalism (but not Western-style democracy). Russia now wanted Western aid, so it was unwilling to use its Security Council veto. At last, the UN seemed free to act as its founders had wished.

Peacekeeping

The ending of the Cold War saw a huge increase in UN observer and peacekeeping missions: two in 1988, three in 1989, four in 1991 and 1992, and five in 1993. In the middle of this period came the first Gulf War (1990–1991). The war was triggered on August 2, 1990, by Iraq, when its leader at the time, Saddam Hussein, ordered the invasion of Kuwait. The next day the UN Security Council called for Iraq to withdraw, but it did not do so. On November 29, the Security Council agreed to the use of force against Iraq unless it withdrew from Kuwait by January 15, 1991. Saddam refused to move his armies. On January 16–17, the first Gulf War began with a massive air attack led by the United States, which provided most of the forces. This was the first time since Korea (see page 14) that an armed force with UN approval had tackled an aggressor head-on.

The U.S.-led attack (named Operation Desert Storm) drove the Iraqis out of Kuwait. The United State's powerful position was a sign of what lay ahead.

U.S. troops in Kuwait during the Gulf War, 1991. As the Iraqi troops withdrew, they set fire to Kuwait's oil fields. One of these can be seen burning in the background. ▼

FACTFILE: Key moments in UN history

1945	UN founded, San Francisco.
1946	General Assembly and Security Council meet in London. Cold War beginning. First secretary-general appointed.
1948	World Health Organization (WHO) set up. General Assembly accepts Universal Declaration of Human Rights.
1956	First UN peacekeeping force (UNEF), for conflict over Suez Canal (see page 15).
1971	Republic of China takes the "China seat" at the UN (see page 15).
1990	UN-approved armed forces fight first Gulf War against Iraq.
1992	Earth Summit in Rio de Janeiro. UNPROFOR enters former Yugoslavia (see pages 4–5).
1995	UN Conference on Women, Beijing, China.
1997	Reform of UN started. Kyoto Summit draws up agreement to halt global warming.
2001	September 11 terrorist attack on New York and the Pentagon. UN backs U.S. "war on terrorism."
2002	World Summit on Sustainable Development in Johannesburg (see page 41) fails to accept effective measures.

Sole superpower

During the Cold War, East-West mistrust had limited the work the UN could do. In the 1990s the UN faced a new problem: a world dominated by one gigantic economic and military superpower, the United States.

U.S. control over the UN came from two sources. First, it provided by far the largest share (22 percent) of the UN budget. By limiting its payments to the UN, the United States could bring the organization to its knees. Second, the United States could use its vast wealth to put pressure on other countries.

U.S. domination meant that only U.S.-approved projects happened. Agreements to help the environment, for example, were useless without U.S. backing (see page 41). Only UN peacekeeping missions accepted by the U.S. went ahead. On the other hand, the U.S. sometimes acts without UN approval. In March 2003 the United States invaded Iraq without UN approval.

As we have seen, the UN's main purpose is to prevent conflicts from breaking out and to bring peace if they do. This raises the tricky question of whether the UN may intervene within an independent state.

One argument says that all states are sovereign, meaning they are entirely responsible for what goes on within their borders. But others argue that some government behavior is so harmful that outsiders must step in to protect the people from their government's actions. These two viewpoints were clearly seen during the Kosovo crisis of 1999.

The Novi Sad oil refinery in the north of Serbia was bombed twice during the NATO attacks in 1999. Here, local residents wait to be ferried to the other shore of the river after an attack. ▼

Kosovo

For generations Kosovo was a province of Serbia, which is now part of Serbia and Montenegro, the former Yugoslavia. The people of Kosovo were mainly Albanian Muslims, but the rest of Serbia was mostly Christian.

Many Kosovo Albanians wanted independence from Serbia. Some tried to drive the Serbs out by force. Then in 1998–1999, there were widespread reports that the Serbs were seriously mistreating the Albanians, trying to make them leave Kosovo (this was known as ethnic cleansing). Negotiations to halt ethnic cleansing failed, and armed forces from NATO (an alliance of the United States and western European nations) attacked the Serb troops and drove them from Kosovo.

NATO's action did not have UN backing, and it split the Security Council. Critics said that NATO, led by the United States, Britain, and France, was breaking the UN Charter by attacking a member state. NATO chiefs said they were acting to prevent a worse crisis. In the end, all the UN could do was provide the Interim Administration Mission in Kosovo to get the province back on its feet after the bloodshed.

Conflict prevention

Rather than face a situation like Kosovo, the UN tries hard to prevent conflicts from breaking out in the first place. It has envoys and special representatives at possible trouble spots around the world who report back to the secretary-general and the Security Council. In 2002, for example, the UN worked hard to ease the tension between the United States and Iraq when the United States accused Iraq of building weapons of mass destruction, such as nuclear or chemical weapons. This did not prove to be successful.

Another UN tactic to prevent conflict is to set up a "thin blue line" of UN troops between opposing forces. This has been done twice, in Macedonia (1992–1999) and the Central African Republic (1998–2000).

"Tired and Lonely
Tired
And lonely,
So tired
The heart aches.
Meltwater trickles
Down the rocks,
The fingers are numb,
The knees tremble.
It is now,
Now, that you must not give in."

Lines written by UN Secretary-General Dag Hammarskjöld in July 1961 while he was trying to tackle a serious crisis in the newly independent Congo

UN Secretary-General Dag Hammarskjöld in 1960 ▶

Peacemaking and peacekeeping

The United Nations has been better at making peace than at stopping war from breaking out. A major reason for its peacemaking success has been the strictly neutral position of the secretaries-general. Not everyone has accepted this neutrality. Once, when speaking to the UN General Assembly, the Soviet leader Nikita Khruschev took off his shoe and hammered it on his desk to emphasize his belief that Secretary-General Dag Hammarskjöld was pro-Western.

Success and failure

The UN had a successful year in 1988. Secretary-General Javier Pérez de Cuéllar played a key part in getting Soviet forces to withdraw from Afghanistan and persuading Iran and Iraq to end their eight-year war. Furthermore, UN peacekeeping forces were awarded the Nobel Peace Prize.

▲ Soviet troops withdraw from Afghanistan in 1988

The UN has successfully brought peace, however, only when doing so has suited all members of the Security Council. The Soviet Union left Afghanistan because it saw little hope of victory, just as the United States had withdrawn their troops from Vietnam in 1972 for similar reasons. In contrast, when Russia invaded the breakaway province of Chechnya in 1994, and when NATO attacked Serbia over Kosovo in 1999, UN peacemaking was ineffective.

Peacekeeping

The original UN Charter did not give the UN a peacekeeping role. But the UN has undertaken peacekeeping missions since 1948, when it sent UNTSO (the UN Truce Supervision Organization) to the Middle East. Its job was to supervise the uneasy truce (cease-fire) between the recently

formed state of Israel and its Arab neighbors. UNTSO's activities have been—and still are—spread over territory within five countries: Egypt, Israel, Jordan, Lebanon, and Syria.

Peacekeeping missions need the approval of the Security Council and the states concerned. They are made up of military personnel, police, and civilians. Since 1945 more than 750,000 people have served as UN peacekeepers. Almost 1,700 have died in this service.

At the beginning of 2003, there were 15 UN peacekeeping operations in the field. UNTSO and UNMOGIP (an observer force set up to watch the tense India-Pakistan border) had been in the field since the 1940s.

Some say UN peacekeeping is a costly waste of time because it does not really keep the peace. As an example, they point to the UN

▲ The UN peacekeeping force remains in Cyprus more than 35 years after it was first sent out. The troops patrol the buffer zone between Greek and Turkish areas.

peacekeeping force in Cyprus (UNFICYP), set up in 1964 to prevent trouble between the Greek and Turkish populations in Cyprus. But ten years later the Turkish army invaded Cyprus, and the UN force was unable to stop bloodshed.

ORGANIZATION IN FOCUS:
Agenda for peace

In 1992 the UN Secretary-General Boutros Boutros-Ghali published a radical paper on UN peacekeeping called "Agenda for Peace." He wanted a Military Staff Committee to advise the Security Council on military matters (an idea first suggested in 1945). More far-reaching, he asked for heavily armed UN "peace enforcement units" to enforce cease-fires. Neither proposal has yet been introduced.

Common interest

In the UN Charter, member states agree to

> "unite our strength to maintain international peace and security ...armed force shall not be used, save [except] in the common interest."

The key phrase here is "common interest." In theory, it means the interest of humanity, of all states. This has been just about impossible to define. However, the lack of

commonality has not stopped the Security Council from sometimes calling for and supporting the use of force.

The Security Council has agreed to the use of military force against or within North Korea (1950, see page 14), Iraq (1990–1991, see page 27), Somalia (1992), Rwanda (1994), Haiti (1994), Albania (1997), and East Timor (1999). All of these countries are small states with few international friends. No country dared object when the permanent members of the Security Council said it was in the "common interest" to intervene in these places. The same

UN forces disembark from their landing craft as they arrive in Somalia, 1992. ▼

applies to countries against which the UN has imposed sanctions, cutting their economic ties with the rest of the world.

Because of the permanent members' veto, the Security Council has never demanded action against a major power. It did not do so when the Soviet Union invaded Hungary (1956), Czechoslovakia (1967), and Afghanistan (1980); nor when Britain and France invaded Egypt (1956); nor when the United States attacked Cambodia (1966), Grenada (1983), and Afghanistan (2001). It never seems to be in the "common interest" to confront a major power.

Enforcement

Although UN peace enforcement has been selective, several of its missions have certainly been worthwhile. The wars in Korea and in the Gulf stopped military governments that had not been elected from getting away with aggression. The UN Transitional Administration in East Timor (1999) helped the newly independent state of East Timor find its feet and defeat rebels and bandits.

There have also been failures. A large U.S.-led task force sent to Somalia in 1992 (UNITAF) withdrew in 1995 after achieving nothing. Far more terrible, the 2,500-strong UN Assistance Mission for Rwanda (UNAMIR) failed to stop the killing of 800,000 people, some of them UNAMIR members, in 1994.

"Speed was of the essence. The nearest available troops were the Austrian and Iranian contingents serving in UNDOF [Israel–Syria] ... They could be transported overland by truck convoy and reach their new deployment [location] within a few hours. However, I could not transfer them without the consent of their governments.

"I first contacted the Austrian government, which let me know that they rather preferred to have their troops stay where they were. So I turned to the ... Shah [of Iran] ... [and] he gave his assent.**"**

Secretary-General Kurt Waldheim on how he gathered a UN force to send to Lebanon, 1979

Disarmament

The appearance of terrible new weapons like machine guns, bombs, and poison gas led to a new idea in peacekeeping; disarmament. It was tried with Germany after World War I (for example, Germany was not allowed to have an air force), and in 1932–1933 the League of Nations held an unsuccessful 60-nation disarmament conference.

▲ Soviet leader Leonid Brezhnev and U.S. President Jimmy Carter meet to discuss the Strategic Arms Limitation Treaty (SALT II) in 1979. The two superpowers negotiated the treaty without UN involvement.

The UN and disarmament

The arrival of nuclear weapons made disarmament more urgent, and it became a major UN issue. The UN cannot demand disarmament; it can only assist the work of member states.

This is done by various UN committees and groups that focus on limiting and abolishing nuclear, chemical, and biological weapons. Recently, the UN Institute for Disarmament Research helped with a convention to ban antipersonnel mines, which was accepted by 109 countries by the end of 2001.

Test ban

The UN works closely with the Conference on Disarmament, which is a negotiating forum attended by many nations, set up by the UN General Assembly in 1978. The conference negotiated the 1993 Chemical Weapons Convention, banning the development, production, stockpiling, and use of chemical weapons, and the 1997 Comprehensive Nuclear-Test-Ban

◄ Weapons of mass destruction. Fitted with a nuclear warhead, the cruise missile is a major part of the West's defense arsenal. It flies very low to avoid detection and can be targeted with great accuracy.

Treaty. Sixty-nine countries have fully accepted this treaty (2002), and 100 satellites are circling Earth to pick up any signs of nuclear activity.

But treaties and test bans do not necessarily make the world safer. In 2002, two countries that have nuclear weapons, India and Pakistan, came close to war. Both countries said that they could not rule out the possibility of using nuclear weapons. The UN could do no more than urge moderation.

Iraq

The Security Council has only once tried to force a country to disarm, in 1991. After a UN-backed force had defeated Iraq in the first Gulf War (see page 18), the UN ordered Iraq to destroy all its means of production, storage, and delivery of weapons of mass destruction (meaning nuclear, chemical, and biological weapons). The UN sent weapons inspectors to see that the resolution was carried out.

Iraq made the inspectors' work as difficult as possible. As a result, the inspectors were withdrawn in 1998 and Britain and the United States launched air strikes against Iraq. In late 2002 the UN passed another resolution calling for the destruction of Iraq's weapons of mass destruction. Weapons inspectors once more returned to Iraq.

FACTFILE: Some UN-backed multinational disarmament agreements

1959	Antarctic Treaty banned weapon testing there.
1963	Treaty allowed nuclear testing only in underground sites.
1967	Latin America and the Caribbean declared free of nuclear weapons.
1968	Treaty outlawed the spread of nuclear weapons.
1972	Biological weapons outlawed.
1985	South Pacific declared free of nuclear weapons.
1993	Chemical weapons outlawed.
1996	Comprehensive Nuclear-Test-Ban Treaty outlawed all nuclear testing.
1997	Convention outlawed antipersonnel mines.

Note: Not all states accept all these agreements.

In the field of human rights, as with disarmament, the UN can do little more than advise, educate, and protest. Yet it is has had marked success in this area. Today, in nearly all parts of the world, groups that are often abused—women, racial minorities, and children—at least know about their human rights. More than any other body, the UN has been responsible for this development.

Definition

Human rights need to be defined before they can be defended. The UN Charter speaks of its "faith in fundamental human rights," and in 1948 the UN wrote its Universal Declaration of Human Rights. The declaration is fully accepted in international law, and some countries have included it in their constitutions.

In 1976 the declaration was backed by the International Covenant on Economic, Social, and Cultural Rights, accepted by 143 states (2001), and another on Civil and Political Rights, accepted by 147 states (2001). Other agreements cover issues like genocide, refugees, racism, women, torture, and children. These and other matters were discussed at the World Conference on Human Rights held in Vienna, 1993. To some people's surprise, the conference caused bitter disputes.

Enforcement

Difficulties at Vienna came largely over two issues. First, if states are sovereign (entirely responsible for what goes on within their borders), what right to outsiders have to interfere in their human rights records? Second, what happens when separate rights conflict with each other? For example, when religious beliefs clash with beliefs about personal freedoms such as the equality of women.

The job of finding answers to such difficulties lies with the UN High Commissioner for Human Rights. The Commissioner for 2002–2006 is Sergio Vieira de Mello, from Brazil.

Veiled women in Kabul, the capital of Afghanistan. When the strict Taliban government was overthrown in 2002, many women gave up their veils, but some chose to continue wearing them. ▼

He and his department work mainly by collecting information and publicizing serious breaches of human rights, and through diplomacy.

Perhaps the biggest success of the human rights campaign was the ending of the racist apartheid regime in South Africa. UN information, sanctions, campaigns, and boycotts of sporting events all played their part. In contrast, the UN failed to take any significant action when, in 1989, Chinese government troops killed hundreds of unarmed people during demonstrations in Beijing's Tiananmen Square.

▲ A lone protester captured the world's attention in 1989 when he stopped a line of tanks in Tiananmen Square, Beijing. Hundreds died and thousands were injured when Chinese troops tried to remove demonstrators protesting against the government.

FACTFILE: Universal Declaration of Human Rights

The first five articles of the Declaration are as follows:

- All human beings are born free and equal in dignity and rights.
- Everyone is entitled to all the rights and freedoms set forth in this Declaration, without distinction of any kind, such as race, color, sex, language, religion, political or other opinion, national or social origin, property, birth, or other status.
- Everyone has the right to life, liberty, and security of person.
- No one shall be held in slavery or servitude; slavery and the slave trade shall be prohibited in all their forms.
- No one shall be subjected to torture or to cruel, inhuman, or degrading treatment or punishment.

29

The law of nations

The United Nations is proud of its record in spreading international law. The reason such law is needed is obvious: It is better to settle a dispute in court than on the battlefield.

The World Court

The International Law Commission represents the world's main legal systems. It makes international law on issues like treaties and state debts. Other bodies set out international law on areas like trade, the environment, and terrorism.

The main court for disputes between countries is the International Court of Justice, or "World Court" (set up in 1946). By the end of 2002, it had heard 122 cases. These covered issues like disputed boundaries, economic rights, and compensation. For instance, when the Iranian government held hostage members of the U.S. embassy in Tehran (1979), the United States took the matter to the World Court. The court ordered Iran to free the Americans, which it eventually did. Normally, states agree before a case is heard to accept the

▲ Judge Lloyd Williams of the International Criminal Tribunal for Rwanda (ICTR). The ICTR was set up to prosecute those responsible for the genocide in Rwanda in 1994. At least half a million people died during thirteen weeks of killing.

court's decision, so enforcing its judgements is not a problem.

International criminal court

After World War II several leaders of Nazi Germany and Japan were found guilty of war crimes and punished, some with death. Since then, international lawyers have argued that there should be a permanent court to try people accused of crimes against humanity.

The International Criminal Tribunal for the Former Yugoslavia (1993) and the International Criminal Tribunal for Rwanda (1994) were steps toward an international criminal court. The Yugoslavia tribunal attracted attention in July 2001 when it accused ex-president Slobodan Milosevic of crimes against humanity. Although Milosevic argued that only a Yugoslavian court could try him, the trial went ahead (October 2002).

In 1998 the UN General Assembly voted to replace temporary tribunals with a permanent international criminal court. The court was due to begin in July 2002, but first it had to be accepted by the Security Council. Here a problem occurred.

The United States was worried that the court might be used to try U.S. military personnel.

The project could go ahead, therefore, only if the Security Council agreed to give certain categories of people immunity from its action. The court judges were inaugurated in March, 2003.

"For nearly half a century… the General Assembly has recognized the need to establish … a court to prosecute and punish persons responsible for crimes such as genocide. Many thought … that the horrors of the Second World War—the camps, the cruelty, the exterminations, the Holocaust—could never happen again. And yet they have. In Cambodia, in Bosnia and Herzegovina, in Rwanda … Genocide … is now a word of our time … a heinous reality that calls for a historic response."

United Nations Secretary-General Kofi Annan, 1998

Ex-president of Yugoslavia Slobodan Milosevic on trial at the International Criminal Tribunal for the Former Yugoslavia, 2001.▼

Women

The former UN High Commissioner for Human Rights, Mary Robinson, has said, "There can be no human rights without women's rights." Few would disagree with this. Even so, an actual case will show how tricky this issue can be.

The veil

In Saudi Arabia, Muslim women must wear a veil covering their faces in public. This law is enforced by men. In 2002 fifteen girls died in a school fire because the male authorities would not let them flee into the street unveiled.

A tragic event like this may seem to highlight clear discrimination against women. If a racial group were treated in this way, there would certainly be a fierce international outcry. The UN might even impose sanctions on the country. This has not happened in the case of Saudi women for three reasons. First, the Saudis say that because their laws come from God, it is not for human beings to question them. To do so would be to undermine the Saudis' right to religious freedom. In other words, religious and women's rights are in conflict.

Second, since Saudi Arabia is the world's largest oil-producing state, oil-consuming nations prefer to turn a blind eye to its human-rights record rather than risk annoying the Saudis.

Finally, Western powers have not questioned the Saudis' record on human rights in part because they need the right-wing Saudi government as an ally against their enemies in the region, notably Iraq.

◄ This Pakistani woman was viciously attacked on the orders of the local village council because she divorced her husband. The crime shocked Pakistan and highlighted abuses against women in rural areas.

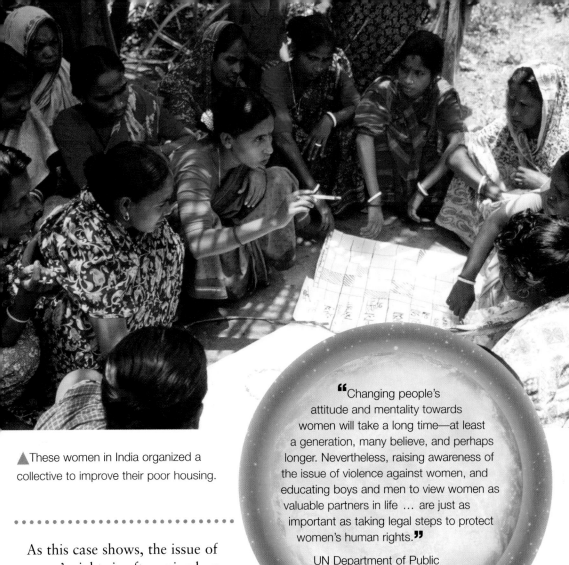

▲These women in India organized a collective to improve their poor housing.

> "Changing people's attitude and mentality towards women will take a long time—at least a generation, many believe, and perhaps longer. Nevertheless, raising awareness of the issue of violence against women, and educating boys and men to view women as valuable partners in life ... are just as important as taking legal steps to protect women's human rights."
>
> UN Department of Public Information, 1996

· ·

As this case shows, the issue of women's rights is often mixed up with ancient custom, other human rights, global politics, and economics.

Successes

Nevertheless, the UN has been successful in improving the lot of women overall. It has done this through the Commission on the Status of Women, the UN Development Fund for Women, and four World Conferences on Women (Mexico City, 1975; Copenhagen, 1980; Nairobi, 1985; Beijing, 1995). As a result, more states have women in positions of high political and administrative responsibility. Thanks largely to the UN and the WHO, the traditional practice of genital mutilation of young girls is declining. Most encouraging of all, almost all countries have accepted the UN target of free primary education for all girls as well as boys.

Chapter Six:
Working Together

About 85 percent of the UN budget is spent by the Economic and Social Council. This organization does valuable work for worldwide development, but it gets much less notice in the media than other UN agencies. Its programs divide roughly into two areas: economic and social.

Economic development

UN economic development aims to close the gap between rich and poor nations. At the start of 2002, nearly half the world's population (mostly people in Africa, Asia, Latin America, and the Caribbean) lived on under $2 per day. In contrast, in the United States a person must live on less than $24 per day to be officially considered poor. Another example of the rich-poor divide is that the British government aims to give half its young people a college education, while more than 1 billion people worldwide are illiterate.

The UN tackles these problems in two ways: by encouraging wealthy states to assist the poorer ones and by giving direct aid. Direct aid may be specialist advice, or grants or loans from the International Monetary Fund (IMF) or the World Bank. The UN Development Programme (UNDP) plans and guides such assistance. The World Bank lends about $25 billion a year. This may seem like a lot, but it is only about a tenth of the total annual income of a medium-sized country like Turkey. Moreover, the country getting the loan has to agree to certain conditions, such as cutting government spending.

Tragically, by the 21st century, many developing countries were spending much of their income on repaying debts rather than on development. In the light of this, the UN backed plans from wealthy countries to cancel the debts of developing countries.

In its early years, the UN welcomed short-term plans for development. By the 1960s this approach was changing because it took no notice of environmental damage. For instance, expanding agriculture by clearing ancient forests brought short-term benefits but caused serious long-term damage. By the 21st century, the UN had turned to sustainable development, the long-term well-being of the earth and its people (see pages 40–41).

Social development

Social development is linked to economic development and to human rights. It covers matters like living conditions, education, health, and population control. By working with national governments, the UN has made the remarkable achievement of slowing the rate of population growth. It is now thought that the world population may begin to fall by 2050.

ORGANIZATION IN FOCUS:
The United Nations and drugs

The UN Drug Control Programme (UNDCP) was set up in 1991 to deal with the international drug problem. It collects information and tries to stop money laundering (putting money earned from drugs into legitimate businesses). It also helps farmers growing drug crops such as coca (used for making cocaine) and opium poppies (used for heroin) to change over to other crops. In 1997, seeing a strong connection between drugs and crime, UNDCP joined with the Centre for International Crime Prevention (CICP) to form a super drug-busting agency, the UN Office for Drug Control and Crime Prevention (ODCCP).

Farmers in Colombia receive chickens as part of a UN crop-substitution program. The plan is to encourage farmers to raise chickens instead of growing drug crops. ▼

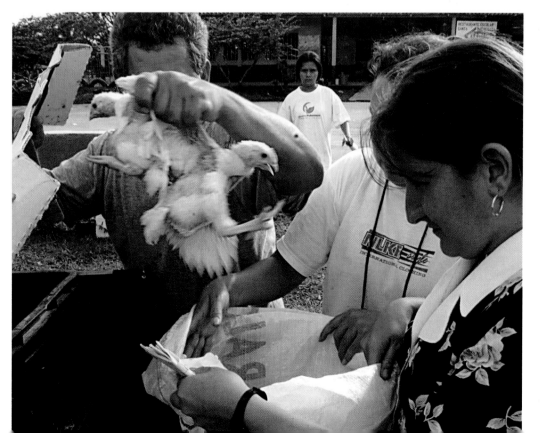

Health and happiness

In some areas of human activity, international cooperation is essential. One of these is health. Disease respects no boundaries, and for very little money many of the health benefits enjoyed in richer countries can be spread to poorer ones.

Many successes

The UN does not often get directly involved with health matters. Normally, it hands them over to agencies, in particular the World Health Organization (WHO).

The WHO's first great triumph was the elimination of smallpox worldwide in 1980. This was achieved by the large-scale immunization of children against the disease. A similar immunization program aims to rid the world of polio by 2005. In 1998, 130 million Indian children were immunized against polio in a single day. Swift

▲ As part of its campaign against smallpox, the WHO organized mass vaccinations in India in 1964. This photo shows a mass vaccination of children in New Delhi.

progress is also being made against diseases such as tetanus, measles, whooping cough, diphtheria, and tuberculosis, saving the lives of an estimated 2.5 million children a year. In Africa campaigns are tackling guinea worm, leprosy, river blindness, and elephantiasis.

Work to be done

Although this work is impressive, much remains to be done. There are two key targets. One is infectious disease, which the WHO combats through immunization and making drugs widely available. The other target is diarrhea and other illness caused by pollution. By providing clean drinking water, the WHO works with UN development agencies to fight diarrhea that kills millions each year.

AIDS

The greatest world health disaster in modern times has been the spread of AIDS. By 2002 about 42 million people were living with the disease, and over 23 million had died from it. The figures are increasing sharply each year.

To face this threat, seven UN agencies came together to set up the Joint UN Programme on HIV/AIDS (UNAIDS). UNAIDS does not tackle the disease itself, but it gives information and does research to support the work of others. In 2002 UNAIDS had a staff of 250 and a budget of $3 billion.

Although its work has been impressive, by 2003 UNAIDS had made little headway. In this field, as in so many others, UN efforts are not enough. In the end, the success of the anti-AIDS campaign will depend on national governments.

"Responses to the AIDS epidemic have shown humanity at both its worst and its best. Denial, blind panic, and victim blaming have been among the worst responses. But gradually, courage, creativity, care, and new reserves of compassion have come to the fore .... Because the impact of AIDS is felt on every continent and in every field of human endeavor, an effective response to AIDS has to be equally broad. It requires all of us to find new ways of working together.**"**

From UNAIDS report "Together We Can"

As part of the AIDS education program these students in Burundi have received T-shirts reminding them of the dangers of AIDS. ▼

A common humanity

The last decade of the 20th century saw a sharp rise in civil wars and natural disasters, particularly flooding. Both had terrible effects—homelessness, hunger, sickness, despair, and death. Yet, as most people also saw on their TV screens, the world community responded to each disaster with swift and generous assistance. The UN was at the heart of each response.

OCHA

When a disaster occurs—for example, the floods that occurred in India in the summer of 2002—dozens of organizations get to work: local government departments, the military, charities, and international relief programs. To prevent the situation from becoming chaotic, the UN has established an Office for the Coordination of Humanitarian Affairs (OCHA) to help everyone involved work together.

▲ As part of the UN coordinated relief effort in Mozambique after terrible floods in 2000, aircraft dropped essential supplies of wheat to isolated communities.

At times of disaster, OCHA works with UN agencies, such as UNICEF, the World Food Programme (which distributes one-third of the world's emergency food), WHO, and the UN High Commissioner for Refugees. OCHA also has plenty of experience working with governments, volunteers, local authorities, religious groups, charities, and all the other relief agencies. It also appeals for funds from around the world.

Statistics give an idea of the scale of the problems that OCHA tries to solve. In 1998 natural disasters killed 50,000 people worldwide and caused $90 billion worth of damage. The following year, millions were made homeless by war—1.2 million in Angola and 850,000 in Kosovo alone. To tackle tragedies such as these, in 2000 OCHA spent $1.4 billion to help 35 million people in 16 countries.

Refugees

Each year the Office of the UN High Commissioner for Refugees (UNHCR) helps more than 20 million refugees. They may be the victims of natural disaster or of wars. Of these, several million are "stateless" people, meaning they have no passports or papers. No country wants them; they belong nowhere. The UN is often the only protector such people have.

The longest-standing refugee problem is in the Middle East, where there are 3.7 million stateless Palestinians. To handle the situation, in 1949 the UN set up a special agency, the UN Relief and Works Agency for Palestinian Refugees in the Middle East.

Palestinian refugee children in a refugee camp in Jordan

ORGANIZATION IN FOCUS: UNRWA

For stateless Palestinians living in Jordan, Lebanon, Syria, the West Bank, and the Gaza Strip, UNRWA is like a mini-government. It distributes loans to small businesses, runs 647 schools and 122 health centers. One of its more prestigious projects is the European Gaza Hospital, a combined program of UNRWA and the European Union.

● ●

One subject has been at the top of the UN list since the 1980s. That topic is the environment, the very life of planet Earth.

Only the UN

The facts are stark. Our world is measurably heating up, sea levels are rising, and the climate is becoming unstable. One-third of the world's population is without electricity, but providing it will add enormously to the emission of the greenhouse gases that most scientists believe cause global warming. Humankind is swiftly wiping out many of the estimated 14 million species (kinds) of living things on the planet. This is destroying the ecological balance that makes human life possible.

The problems are gigantic. They require a change not just in the way many of us behave but also in the way we think. Programs put in place by individual countries are not enough. The only plan that will work is complete and total international cooperation. Therefore, as the most important body representing the whole of humankind, the UN has to take the lead.

The UN Environment Programme

The UN set up its Environment Programme (UNEP) in 1972. Eleven years later, a General Assembly commission proposed the idea of sustainable development,

● ●

This area of rain forest in Madagascar has been cleared to make space for a cattle ranch. Madagascar's rain forest is being cleared at an alarming rate, threatening species such as lemurs found only on the island. ▼

economic development that does not use up the earth's resources. This has since become a key plank in UN development programs.

Ultimately, the aim is for the whole world to accept sustainable development. This was agreed on (as Agenda 21) at the first Earth Summit, held in Rio de Janeiro in 1992.

Kyoto and beyond

Agreeing on action was one thing. Putting theory into practice has been quite another. By 1997, when a second major environmental conference was held in Kyoto, Japan, little had been done. At Kyoto, however, a firm plan to save the environment (the Kyoto Protocol) was drawn up. Within ten to twelve years, for instance, developed countries would reduce their output of greenhouse gases to 5 percent below the 1990 level.

It all seemed splendid. There were, however, two massive drawbacks. One was that the Kyoto plan was not a treaty; no one had to follow it. Second, the United States, the world's largest polluter, and user of resources, refused to accept the plan.

Another World Summit in Johannesburg in 2002 did not move forward significantly from Rio. The United States, and other countries like Australia and Canada, did not want the summit to agree to new targets and timetables. In most cases they managed

▲ Supplying communities with clean water is a major part of the UN's sustainable development program. The South African government has installed supplies of clean water for more than 7 million people through standpipes like this one in Cape Town.

to prevent these actions A world plan for affordable, renewable energy by 2015 was blocked by a group of countries with large oil and gas reserves. However, agreement was reached to halve the number of people without safe drinking water by 2015.

41

Chapter Eight:
Future Uncertain

●●●●●●●●●●●●●●●●●●●●●●●●●●●●●●●●●

The United Nations has always been criticized. Complaints come under four broad headings: powerlessness, wastefulness, lack of accountability, and double standards.

Powerless

The UN is accused of being powerless because, like the League of Nations, it can pass resolutions but cannot enforce them. This has been seen on dozens of issues, from the environment to weapons control.

In the end, military and financial power rests with national governments. The UN is simply their meeting place. As we saw with the Kyoto Protocol (page 41), it can achieve almost nothing without the backing of state governments.

Wasteful

Until the 1990s the UN budget grew every year. By the 1970s major

▲ Boutros Boutros-Ghali rejected the U.S. charge that the UN was wasteful and refused to cut costs.

●●●●●●●●●●●●●●●●●●●●●●●●●●●●●●

contributors, particularly the United States, were complaining that vast sums were being wasted. In certain areas this was true. In some poorer countries a post as a UN delegate in New York was seen to mean high expenses and little work. Some UN projects, notably those of UNESCO, were criticized as unnecessary.

ORGANIZATION IN FOCUS: UNESCO

In the 1970s people with anti-Western views took control of UNESCO. Its Senegalese Director-General, Amadou-Mahtar M'Bow, said there was no true freedom of the press. Almost all news was distorted, he claimed, because it was provided by Western-owned organizations. The United States, which paid 25 percent of UNESCO's budget, was furious about funding attacks on its own system. It demanded reform of UNESCO. M'Bow refused. In response, in 1984 the United States left UNESCO and even considered leaving the UN itself.

During the 1990s the United States withdrew from UNESCO and refused to agree to Boutros Boutros-Ghali's reappointment as secretary-general (see page 12). It also demanded that the UN bring its spending under control. This was done when Secretary-General Kofi Annan froze its budget in 1997.

Accountable

UN delegates are appointed, not elected. Although in theory they represent the people of the world, those people cannot fire them if they disagree with their decisions or actions. Some say the UN would work better if its main positions—membership of the General Assembly and the Security Council—were elected. Only then would these organizations reflect the true wishes of the people of the world.

Double standards

Recently there have been complaints that the UN has different rules for different countries. This comes from the fact that a handful of rich and powerful states (notably the permanent members of the Security Council) control much UN activity. The Israel-Iraq situation is a common example. It is said that Israel, an ally of the United States,

▲ Iraqis in Baghdad sit under a large mural of former dictator Saddam Hussein. Some people believe that punishing Iraq for breaking UN resolutions is unfair, since other countries have done the same and not been penalized.

often ignores UN resolutions. Yet when Iraq, an enemy of the United States, does so, it is punished.

43

▲ Despite the UN's problems, its headquarters in New York remain a symbol of global cooperation.

Real achievements

For all the criticism of the United Nations, countries still wish to join and play their part, more or less enthusiastically, in its work. There are currently 191 members, and not one has left.

The UN can be justly proud of real achievements. Near the top of the list comes the WHO's work in limiting and even getting rid of disease. In many cases UN peacekeepers have kept opposing sides apart, and its advisers and administrators often help states get back on their feet after disasters. Millions of refugees and people hit by natural disasters owe their well-being, even their lives, to UN workers. The UN has also helped define and spread the system of international law.

As well as these achievements, the UN leads many areas of research. It gathers statistics and informs people about the world and its peoples. One of the best examples is the information gathering of the Global Resource Information Database (GRID), a branch of UNEP. The environmental crisis cannot be dealt with without data, and GRID, working in over 175 states, is a fair, reliable, and scientific data source.

A forum

Less obvious is the UN's role as a forum. In the General Assembly and the Security Council, disagreements can be aired in an orderly and regulated way. When countries show their differences merely by shouting and passing angry resolutions, instead of fighting, the UN's contribution to peace is very real.

The only way

We live in a "global village" that needs global supervision. Our business and industry are global, our sport and recreation are global, our culture is increasingly global, and our greatest problems—poverty, conflicts and wars, the threat of nuclear war, and damage to the environment—are also global.

It is no longer possible for a country to exist and act in isolation from others. We act together or perish together, and the United Nations is our only organization for multinational, worldwide action. It needs to be made more efficient, perhaps. It could also be reorganized to give all members a greater say in what it does. This would give it more authority. Nevertheless, whatever its weaknesses, there is no better alternative to the world's only international forum, the United Nations.

"The United Nations has no independent military capability and very modest funds. Its influence derives from the force of the values it represents, its role in helping to set and sustain global norms and international law, its ability to stimulate global concern and action, and the trust inspired by its practical work on the ground to improve people's lives. The effectiveness of the United Nations in all of these endeavors depends on partnerships ... most of all among peoples, reaching across the lines that might otherwise divide."

UN Secretary-General
Kofi Annan, 2000

New York Mayor Rudi Giuliani discussing terrorism at the UN General Assembly in October 2001, after the September 11 attacks. UN members have widely differing opinions of what counts as terrorism. The UN provides a forum where these differing views can be aired. ▼

Special Note:

Many of the names of organizations and programs in this book have spellings that may be unfamiliar to you, for example, "programme" instead of "program." This is because the UN is an international organization and so uses the British spelling of certain words.

ORGANIZATIONS AND ACRONYMS

UNEP UN Environment Programme

UNESCO UN Educational, Scientific, and Cultural Organization

UNHCR UN High Commissioner for Refugees

UNICEF UN Children's Fund

UNPROFOR UN Protection Force (former Yugoslavia)

WHO World Health Organization

World Bank UN organization established to assist world economic development, primarily through loans

WORDS

accountability able to be held responsible for something

antipersonnel mine mine designed to blow up people rather than tanks or other vehicles

apartheid literally, "living apart," the system of separation and discrimination between races that operated in South Africa until 1994

arbitrate act as a go-between to help negotiation

boycott withdraw from something as a way to protest against it

broker to bring about an agreement between parties

budget statement of income and spending

bureaucrat person who works for a government or similar organization

capitalism economic system in which individuals use their own capital (money) to buy and sell things for a profit

cease-fire suspension of active fighting

charter list of principles and regulations

civil war war fought by different sides within a country

Cold War period of tension between communist states (led by the USSR) and democratic-capitalist states (led by the United States), 1946–1990

communist government on behalf of the people that puts public needs before private rights

covenant solemn undertaking

delegation group sent by a larger body to act on its behalf

diplomacy international discussion and negotiation

economy country's finances, services, and industry

executive decision making and action taking

fascism political belief featuring extreme nationalism and belief in an all-powerful leader

forum place for meeting and discussion

Gaza Strip land on the Mediterranean coast captured and occupied by Israel in 1966

genocide killing, or trying to kill, an entire ethnic group

greenhouse gases gases such as carbon dioxide suspended in the earth's atmosphere that act like the glass of a greenhouse, trapping the sun's heat

ideology belief or thinking; a set of guiding principles

illiterate unable to read or write

mediate to go between parties in a dispute to help them sort out their differences

Middle East countries in Southwest Asia and North Africa usually considered as including countries from Libya in the west to Afghanistan in the east

nationalism passionate belief in the superiority of one's native country above all others

parliament name for some government assemblies; the U.S. government body is called the Congress

proliferation spread

protocol agreement between states

radical (adjective) far-reaching, fundamental; (noun) someone who seeks fundamental change

republic state with an elected head of government

resolution agreement or decision

sanctions measures, such as cutting off trade, to harm a country

sovereign independent, self-governing

summit meeting of major decision makers

sustainable development economic development that does not use up the earth's resources

treaty written agreement between states

tribunal lower, less formal law court

unanimous everyone agreeing

veto stop something from being carried out

FURTHER READING

Gorman, Robert F. *Great Debates at the United Nations: An Encyclopedia of Key Issues, 1945–2000*. Westport, Conn.: Greenwood, 2001.

Melvern, Linda. *World Organizations: United Nations*. Danbury, Conn.: Scholastic, 2001.

Ross, Stewart. *The United Nations*. Chicago: Heinemann, 2002.

USEFUL ADDRESSES

United Nations Headquarters
First Avenue at 46th Street
New York, NY 10017
www.un.org

Office of the High Commissioner for Human Rights
8-14 Avenue de la Paix
1211 Geneva 10, Switzerland
www.unhchr.ch